MW00475868

The Spiritual Impact of Sexual Abuse

Diane Langberg

New
Growth
Press

newgrowthpress.com

New Growth Press, Greensboro, NC 27401
newgrowthpress.com
Copyright © 2017 by Diane Langberg

Unless otherwise indicated, Scripture quotations are taken from the *Holy Bible, English Standard Version.*® Copyright © 2000; 2001 by Crossway Bibles, a division of Good News Publishers. Used by permission. All rights reserved.

Cover Design: Trish Mahoney, themahoney.com

ISBN: 978-1-945270-65-9 (Print)
ISBN: 978-1-945270-66-6 (eBook)

Library of Congress Cataloging-in-Publication Data

Names: Langberg, Diane, author.
Title: The spiritual impact of sexual abuse / Diane Langberg.
Description: Greensboro, NC : New Growth Press, 2017.
Identifiers: LCCN 2017038755| ISBN 9781945270659 (single) | ISBN 9781945270673 (5-pk)
Subjects: LCSH: Adult child sexual abuse victims--Pastoral counseling of. | Sexual abuse victims--Religious life. | Trust in God--Christianity. | Traumatism.
Classification: LCC BV4463.5 .L385 2017 | DDC 261.8/3272--dc23
LC record available at https://lccn.loc.gov/2017038755

Printed in India

30 29 28 27 26 25 24 23   5 6 7 8 9

Those in the counseling field are talking more and more about what is called "meaning-making."[1] The concept originated in Victor Frankel's *Man's Search for Meaning* and refers to the process of how people make sense of knowledge, relationships, and self. Trauma of any kind has the capacity to shape meaning in a person's life. For example, a boy who grows up in an urban setting in poverty, with an abusive, alcoholic father, who experiences a cycle of homelessness due to his drug-addicted mother, and who has been raped by some men in the neighborhood has a life meaning and purpose shaped by trauma: Life is chaotic and disordered; no one can be trusted. Get what you can when you can and watch your back unceasingly.

On the other hand, trauma can shatter meaning. A young girl grows up in an intact home, nurtured and cared for with many developmental opportunities and goes off to the college of her choice. One evening on the way back from the library she is violently, brutally raped. The meaning and purpose she has for her life is now destroyed. Nothing makes sense, trust is eradicated, and the meaning held to by the urban youth now makes more sense to her than her own.

When a situation is destructive to familiar, comfortable beliefs, a person's distress level is high. When someone's pre-trauma beliefs and meaning are resilient and have the capacity to include trauma, suffering, and injustice, the ability to weather the trauma without destruction of meaning and purpose is much higher. The adherence to rigid, pessimistic, or incoherent meanings, particularly those that assume protection from all suffering, seem to prolong trauma symptoms and leave one vulnerable to chronic PTSD. Therefore, it is critical that we grasp some of what sexual abuse in particular does to the meaning and purpose of a child victim and the adult they become, as well as what is involved in helping them find true meaning and purpose not based on pretending the trauma never happened or that it did not really hurt.

Sexual abuse has a spiritual impact. Let's consider this impact specifically as well as what responses might be helpful. There are three things to keep in mind as we seek to both understand abuse and minister to survivors of this childhood trauma. The first is that much of a survivor's thinking is "frozen" in time. A woman who was chronically abused by her father for fifteen years thinks about herself, her life, and her relationships through the grid of the abuse. She may have encountered situations where people proved trustworthy, but she does not trust. She may have heard thousands of words about how God loves her, but the abuse has led her to believe she is trash and an exception to the rule. Trauma stops growth because it shuts everything down. It brings a sense of death. The input from many other experiences, relationally and spiritually, often does not seem to impact the thinking that originated within the context of the abuse.

Second, the abuse occurred to a child, not an adult. Children think concretely, not abstractly. Children learn about abstract concepts like trust, truth, and love from the concrete experiences they have with significant others in their lives. They learn what love is by how Mommy and Daddy treat them. They learn about trust by the trustworthiness, or lack of it, in Mommy and Daddy. In essence, they learn about intangible things, ideas, and values through the tangible. If those who teach them are repeatedly untrustworthy, cruel, hurtful, and lying, then to grasp the meaning of concepts like trust, safety, love, and truth seem like an exercise in the ridiculous. Children can be impacted in these ways not just by sexual abuse but by domestic violence, by physical abuse, by ongoing verbal and emotional abuse, by neglect, and by addictions and rage in the home. They make meaning out of their life experiences.

Third, not only do children think concretely; they learn about the abstract by way of the concrete, adults are also taught about the unseen through the seen. We are of the earth, earthy. God teaches us eternal truths through things in the natural world. We grasp a bit of eternity by looking at the sea. We get a glimmer of infinity by staring into space. We learn about the shortness of time by the quick disappearance of a vapor. Jesus taught us eternal truths the same way. He said he was the bread, the light, the living water, and the vine. We look at the seen and learn about the unseen. Consider the sacraments—water, bread, and wine. We are taught about the holiest of all through the diet of a peasant. This method is also used to understand the character and nature of God himself. God in the flesh, God with skin on, came in the person of Jesus. God explains himself to us through the temporal.

If we consider the combined impact of these factors, we see that many survivors exhibit this quality of thinking frozen in time in that they learned repeatedly through the concrete how to think about the abstract, and they learned repeatedly through the seen what to believe about the unseen. One area that this profoundly impacts is the spiritual. God is viewed through the lens of abuse. Who he is and what he thinks about the survivor is understood based on who Daddy was, or Mommy, or a grandfather, or a youth pastor, or whoever. They have learned about love, trust, hope, faith, through the experience of sexual abuse. They have also learned about the unseen through the visible. The ins and outs of ordinary life have taught them many lessons about who they think God is. That is why a therapist or pastor may have the experience of speaking the truths of Scripture to a survivor, truths desperately needed, and yet finding that they seem to have no impact. The truths and principles don't sink in. Many times survivors can speak eloquently of the truths of Scripture, but on an experiential level their lives are lived out in the context of what the abuse taught them. Intellectually, truth is rooted in the Word of God. Experientially, or personally applied, the truth is rooted in the lessons of abuse.

Sometimes, of course, we find an exception. God has worked miraculous stories of transformation in survivors' lives. Complete about-face changes, however, are few and far between. Consider an article in *The Philadelphia Inquirer* about a young man from Bosnia whose life was touched profoundly by the war there. He wrote an essay about a friend who found his dead mother, and said the following:

> "Her body was white because the grenade that struck her apartment turned the wall into a fine white powder. . . . He kissed his mother before they covered her, and then he went into a small nearby room. *He needed to get away from her so he could think she was still alive.* He needed to believe in that because he needed time. Although he used that time in self-deceit, he needed that time to get carried down to the reality slowly."[2]

Oftentimes survivors can hold on to their belief in God because they are doing what this young man did—they are living in self-deceit. "It was not really abuse." "It wasn't that bad." "He didn't mean it." In other words, "I can believe God is really alive, or truly loves me, because I have in essence 'gone to a nearby room' away from the abuse."

For many survivors of sexual abuse, two irreconcilable realities exist: the reality of a God who says he is both loving and a refuge for the weak, and the reality of their ongoing sexual violation. Each reality seems to cancel out the other, yet both exist. Again, the human mind can manage either alternative—the sexual abuse of a child and no God, or God and protection from sexual abuse. What is one to do with the rape of a child *and* the reality of God? Most survivors will come down on one side or the other. They have faced the rape and God is not to be trusted. Or they hang on tightly to God and the rape is a blip on the screen. The dilemma is not easily solved.

Let's make sure that we grasp the profound impact of ongoing abuse to a child's understanding of God by considering some specific examples.

Sarah is five. Her parents drop her off at Sunday school every week. She has learned to sing, "Jesus loves me, this I know, for the Bible tells me so. Little ones to him belong. They are weak, but he is strong." Sarah's daddy rapes her several times a week. Sometimes she gets a break because he rapes her eight-year-old sister instead. The song says that Jesus loves her. It says that he is strong. So she asks Jesus to stop her daddy from hurting her and her sister. Nothing happens. Maybe Jesus isn't so strong after all, she concludes. Or at least not as strong as Daddy. Nothing, not even Jesus, can stop Daddy. The people who wrote the Bible must not have known about her daddy.

What does incest teach about fathers? That they are untrustworthy. That they have a great deal of power. They are unpredictable. They inflict pain on those they are supposed to care for. They betray, they abandon, deceive, use, and rip you apart. They speak love and reassuring words and then suddenly abuse. God as Father is terrifying.

Michael went away to overnight camp at age seven. He was scared and homesick. His counselor paid him special attention. It made him feel important. But then it got strange and scary. The counselor would teach the Bible study at night and then take Michael for a walk and make him do things he didn't like.

What does abuse teach about God? The natural conclusion of the abused child is that he is cruel, impotent, or uncaring. He does not hear, or if he hears, he does not answer. He thinks children are expendable. He does not keep his word. He is not who he says he is. That since he says he is powerful—distance is wise. Trust is out of the question.

What does the survivor learn about herself? That she is unworthy, trash. She is not loved and probably never will be and her prayers are useless. She brings evil to people or makes them do evil things. No effort on her part brings change.

What does the survivor learn about things like trust and faith? Those are things you never do unless you are an idiot. Love? Love is a word you use when you want to make someone do something they do not want to do. Hope? Hope is a setup. Nothing ever changes anyway.

Emotions Accompanying Traumatic Memory

The trauma of sexual abuse brings out all sorts of emotion with which the Christian community is largely uncomfortable and often condemns. It is important to understand this as we move on to consider how to respond to the spiritual impact of abuse. Abuse results in fear, anxiety, anger, and grief—emotions the church is often not adept at handling head-on. Because the Bible speaks to the resolution and resolve of these emotions, we think that the best way to speak to someone experiencing them is to hurl verses like projectiles at a victim in an attempt to make these feelings go away as quickly as possible. If you are going to enter into the suffering of those who have been traumatized, you have to learn how to sit with and listen to fear, anger, and great grief with compassion and understanding. You will also have to learn how to do it for far longer than you prefer.

Many who are traumatized will be afraid to face and feel the emotions related to the trauma. They fear losing control of themselves and enduring more pain and suffering. These fears are understandable, for the feelings surrounding the trauma are powerful, and such emotions can quickly re-create the trauma in which the survivor felt overwhelmed and helpless. It feels safer to let oneself down into the emotions of the wound in small bites and in the presence of someone who will listen, normalize, and not condemn. Dealing with and healing from such feelings will never occur in a straight line. Feelings will fluctuate between numbness and exhaustion. Those breaks are necessary and must not be rushed.

One practical thing you can do for the trauma survivor who is wrestling with these overwhelming emotions is encourage them to do restorative things with safe people in their lives. Going for a walk and making a note of the beauty that is seen, listening to music, or participating in aerobic exercise (especially when anger and agitation are present) are recommended. These activities can help quiet the mind and rest the body. Doing them with someone who feels stable and safe is also restorative, giving the message that strong feelings have not isolated them as they did during the abuse.

A survivor's anger can be toward others, especially the perpetrators and silent bystanders or anyone seen as responsible for their loss. Anger can also be expressed in guilt and self-blame. The child mind is egocentric and so often the victim rages against herself for being abused. The older sibling who believed she should be able to protect her younger sister from sexual abuse and failed will struggle with guilt. Seeing the self as damaged goods and carrying great shame can bring on self-loathing.

Abuse brings grief, and it can take several forms. Grief can manifest because a childhood is lost, a way of life is gone, a hoped-for home is absent, or a safe parent, or a hoped-for future have disappeared. Many have lost the faith they had in life or in human nature. Another aspect to grief is the sense of powerlessness that pervades. Not only were survivors helpless to stop the trauma, they are helpless to restore what— and who—is gone. You cannot resurrect the dead, nor restore a lost limb, nor retrieve a lost person or an inno- cent childhood. Our sense of power in this world may be largely delusional, but nonetheless we grieve when we lose it.

One characteristic of dealing with survivors of trauma is the repetitious nature of that work. Survivors will say the same things over and over: "How could my father do that to me?" They will be repetitious in dealing with their emotions: "I am so angry that . . ." And they will repeat their losses again and again: "I cannot believe so-and-so is dead . . ." Expect it, and learn to sit with it. The magnitude of the trauma is so great that repetition is necessary. The mind cannot imagine what happened. It cannot hold such a thought. Bearing the intensity of emotions is impossible and so the feelings must be tried on again and again. These are attempts to bear what cannot be borne. They are struggles to integrate into life what does not fit because there are no categories. Be patient, and then be patient some more.

Developing the Heart of God

The essence of working with trauma survivors is about bearing witness to their story and suffering, entering into their life and demonstrating in the flesh the heart of our God toward them and the evil they experienced. If we have not personally come to know and understand the heart of our God in response to evil and suffering, we will either avoid entering into the experience of evil in our client's lives or we will glibly apply the words of Scripture without an accurate representation of the God of Scripture. This work will expose to you the egocentricity of your own heart. You may find you are not so much touched by evil, sin, and suffering in this world and the hearts of human beings unless it infringes on your world, your comfort, and your relationships. You may work hard to keep at a distance the evil, sin, and suffering that do not touch your world. It is disturbing, messy, and inconvenient.

God has used the work I do as a psychologist as a corrective measure in my own life. I have worked with many kinds of people—people I would otherwise have had no contact with. I have seen things like abuse, suicide, terror, torment, psychosis, trauma, obsessions, and wordless grief. Such experiences were not mine; they belonged to other people. They were brought to me, however, and I was invited in. Entering into such things has disturbed my thinking, my feelings, and my sleep. I have had to change my mind about things I was sure were true and ask questions I thought had been finally answered.

Because of my work as a counselor, God is slowly increasing my sensitivity to and awareness of my own sin. Such a growing awareness is frankly, rather uncomfortable. If the truth is told, however, many of the things God does in our lives are uncomfortable. Unfortunately, I tend to also be more aware of the sins of others. That is problematic on two counts. One, it means I am then inclined to sin in my attitudes toward them with judgment, criticism, or arrogance. Two, it means I cannot, if I am to truly love, ignore such things. Discernment of wrong in the life of another is always a call to intercession and sometimes to involvement. It is truthfully easier not to see; it is easier to anesthetize myself with the narcotic of self-deception. However, the dealings of God the Father with his Son on the cross demonstrate for us the evil of sin. To ignore it or dilute it anywhere, including in our own lives, is to refuse his point of view. To accept his point of view is to often feel weighed down by the burden that comes. When the eyes of the heart face the truth of things as they actually are and face sin, our own and others', from God's point of view, we will cry, "God, be merciful to me, a sinner" and with David, "How long, O Lord, how long?"

Thirdly I have been reminded again how much sin is the antithesis of humility. I am aware that there has been a lot of twisted teaching in Christian circles about pride and humility. Humility has been seen as something equivalent to self-hatred and, in fact, ends up being an obsessive focus on the self, which is certainly not what true humility looks like. We have seen many lives destroyed by the church's wrong teaching on humility. We have also had years of a focus on self-esteem, a term that has often been poorly defined and misused. I have been struck by Roy Baumeister's statement: "The most potent recipe for violence is a favorable view of oneself that is disputed or undermined by someone else—in short, threatened egotism."[3] He is saying that people are inclined to do violence or evil when another contradicts their inflated view of themselves.

In Isaiah 14 we read about Lucifer, star of the morning, the shining one. He has fallen, and that fall occurred when he said, "I will ascend above the heights of the clouds; I will make myself like the Most High" (Isaiah 14:14). I think it would be safe to say that God threatened Lucifer's favorable view of himself, and surely we could say violence was the result! He then appears in the garden and says to the humans there, "Indeed, has God said, 'You shall not eat from any tree in the garden'?" When Eve corrects him and says no, only one particular tree he says the following, "You shall not surely die! For God knows that in the day you eat from it your eyes will be opened, and *you will be like God*, knowing good and evil" (Genesis 3:4–5, italics added). There is the phrase again, "like God." It is a subtle twist of the truth. We were created *in the image of* God. The goal Satan offered was close to the real goal. It had to be or it would not have been capable of deceiving.

The problem came when Adam and Eve left their position as creatures dependent on the wisdom of the Father. They thought they were ascending and assumed a rather inflated view, which God threatened, and violence resulted. Whenever we wiggle out of our position as creature, dependent on our Father, and elevate ourselves, violence, sin, and evil will result. We still, like our forbearers, want to know good and evil. We still do not like our position as creatures, dependent, finite, and frail. We are often insulted that God will not explain things to us. We are impatient with him because he has not told us enough.

He has said, "In the world you have tribulation" (John 16:33). He has said, "The whole world lies in the power of the evil one" (1 John 5:19). He has said, "For I, the LORD, do not change" (Malachi 3:6). And he has told us the goal—that we should be conformed to the image of Christ, be creatures that look like him. He has made the result plain, but he has kept the working out of that result mysterious.

How hard it is, in this time and place, with sin and suffering rampant in us and around us, to bow the knee and acknowledge ourselves as creatures and Jesus Christ as Lord. I believe we can trust him and bow in humility because I have seen something of the heart of God. The cross of Christ is the manifestation of the heart of God in time and space. The cross of Christ is where our two seemingly irreconcilable realities, sin and God, come together. The cross of Christ is where God and sin crash together—and the crash is on the heart of God himself.

He bore the slaveries of this world, the child prostitution, the inquisitions, the racial injustice, the Holocaust, Rwanda, Bosnia, Uganda, the Khmer Rouge, the Black Plague, AIDS, Ground Zero, the suffering in our bodies and sickness in our souls. My friends, he knows our griefs and carried our sorrows. He was wounded for our transgressions and by his stripes we are healed. He was wounded and crushed for our sins. It was God's good plan to crush him and fill him with grief. Yet when his life is made an offering for sin, he will have a multitude of children, many heirs. When he sees all that is accomplished by his anguish, he will be satisfied. Because of what he has experienced, he will make it possible for man to be counted righteous. He will be given the honors of one who is mighty and great because he exposed himself to death. He was counted among those who are sinners. He bore the sins of many and interceded for sinners (Isaiah 53).

As you wrestle with evil, sin, and suffering, let *this* be a sign unto you—you shall find the Redeemer robbed of his clothes and hanging on the cross. He compels us to notice him and to note what he allows his enemies to do to him.[4] Let us sit there and see. The cross speaks. Have we sat and listened?

He was made the subject of shame as absolutely as was the custom in that day. Grace abandoned him. In other words, he descended into hell. The Creator is destroyed. Life becomes dead. Glory turns to shame. Beauty is obliterated. Living water thirsts. All Power becomes powerless. The great Clothier of everything is stripped naked. All-Honor is despised. Holiness becomes excrement. Love is forsaken. Heaven enters hell. These truths mean many wonderful, eternal things. They also mean that our God understands trauma.

A young Japanese man, who teaches conducting at a university and came to Christ through listening to Bach's cantatas, recently taught us something beautiful based on Bach's Cantata for the 19th Sunday after Trinity. One of the arias reads like this: "I will the cross-staff gladly carry; it comes from God's loving hand. It leads me after my torments to God, into the promised land." The German word *Kreuzstab* means cross-staff.

He said Bach is portraying the cross as both an instrument of crucifixion and the staff we lean on.

Certainly we think of it as the instrument of death. There our Savior died and sin died with him. That means sin can die in us so the life of God can be borne in us. We see the suffering and grief Christ bore for us. We see the sicknesses, all the sicknesses of this world, borne in that one body. He did that so that all of those things might die forever. But is it not also the staff on which we lean? Where else can we go when our own sin horrifies us and yet we cannot stop? Where else can we go when sickness, sorrow, and grief overwhelm us? Does not the cross sustain us in such times? As I bow before God and allow him to produce his viewpoint in me, several things will result.

First, I will know without question that evil is not just "out there"; it is also "in here." I will never see the world as divided between "them" and "us." There is no "them" because we are all "them." God's point of view will lead me to hate sin wherever I find it, including in myself. When I understand that it is the excrement of human souls, I will respond as he did. I will go to any lengths to see it killed, both in me and in this world. I will rather endure suffering than sin against a holy God.

Second, those who are suffering will know that I will give time and compassion because I am called to identify with the sufferings of Christ. To evade them is to evade him. What I do to the least, I have done to him. I will understand that I will never encounter any human suffering that Christ has not borne. He has carried every kind of suffering you find. When I sit with those who suffer, I sit with him. I will understand that God would assuage the anguish of this world through his people. Wherever creation groans, the method of healing its deep wounds and assuaging its convulsive grief is by planting the children of God in its midst. Wherever men and women of God live, *there* is some measure of healing the world's wounds and soothing its sorrow. The weeping of girls and women, boys and men in the dark and cruel places of this earth is heard and healed by the living presence of the Word of God in the lives of those *who incarnate what they say they believe.* We "comfort those who are in any affliction with the comfort with which we ourselves are comforted by God" (2 Corinthians 1:4).

Third, I will walk this world with humility. Humility will come because I know that with the sinfulness of my own soul I can never point a finger, raise my head in arrogance, or react with impatience to a struggling sinner. Humility will come because I know I am a finite and frail creature that is utterly dependent on my Creator for life and godliness. Humility will come because I follow in the footsteps of the Servant of servants.

Finally, I will be wise to discern truth from error. Wisdom will come because I know the cross of Christ must be central in all my thinking. Wisdom will come because I make a practice of forcing my mind to think through what it so readily and comfortably accepts. Wisdom will come because I know keenly my use of the narcotic of self-deception.

The Response to the Sufferer

You and I become the representative of God to the survivor. Our work is to teach in the seen that which is true in the unseen. Our words, tone of voice, actions, body movements, responses to rage, fear, failure all become ways that the survivor learns about God. I believe the reputation of God himself is at stake in our lives. We are called to represent him well.

While we try to represent God, the survivor struggles with questions about God: Who is he? What does he think about my abuse, my rape, the loss of all things? What does he think about me? Am I loved? Am I forgivable? Does his patience run out? Why should I have hope?

In this case, words are initially meaningless. What are words when you grew up hearing "Daddy loves you," and then Daddy raped you. Or when your grandfather called you over to sit on his lap, and when you were afraid he said not to worry because this time it would be okay, but it never was. When the therapist says, "This is a safe place," the survivor responds "Right." "Oh, sure." Or she may have become so desperate that words are believed no matter what actions might suggest, making it easy for her to be abused again.

Our task is no less than living out before them the character of God himself. Early in my work with survivors I longed for a woman who had been chronically abused to truly know the love of God. I tried telling her about it but realized that she was only politely listening.

I clearly remember getting down on my knees before God and begging him to help her see what she so desperately needed to see—that he loved her. What I heard back from God was "You want her to know how much I love her? Then you go love her in a way that demonstrates that. You want her to know that I am trustworthy and safe? Then you go be trustworthy and safe." Demonstrate in the flesh the character of God over time so that who you are reveals God to the survivor.

That, of course, is the incarnation, isn't it? Jesus, in the flesh, explaining God to us. Jesus, bringing the unseen down into flesh and blood actualities. The survivor needs us to incarnate God for two reasons. One, we all need that. Secondly, this need is intensified for the trauma victim because what has been repeatedly taught to a child in the seen is the antithesis of the truth of God. She has learned about fathers, power, trust, love, and refuge from one who emulated the father of lies.

If you want the survivor to understand that God is a refuge, then be one for her. If you want her to grasp the faithfulness of God, then be faithful to her. If you want her to understand the truthfulness of God, then never lie to her. If you want her to understand the infinite patience of God, then be patient with her. And where you are not a refuge, or are tired of being faithful, or are fudging in your answers or growing impatient with the necessary repetition, then get down on your knees and ask God to give you more of himself so that you might represent him well.

The second aspect of the response is to speak truth. When people have experienced interpersonal evil, especially as children, they carry deeply embedded lies within. Such lies need to be exposed, gently and slowly, so the light of the truth can take their place. There are usually particular aspects of certain memories that burned those lies into the brain and help keep them there. For example, a woman who was sadistically abused during childhood told of being forced to kill a loved pet or risk further pain. She was told repeatedly that she was evil and no one would ever love her. Her vivid memory of killing her pet and the blood on her hands provided tangible proof of her evil and burned that lie into her brain. It took a long, long time of carefully picking our way through that memory and all its pieces for her to even begin to grasp the subtlety and hideousness of the lies it had taught her.

This can happen in any kind of trauma. It is prevalent in combat vets—particularly when they experience moral injury, e.g., they participate in or bear witness to things that violate conscience; things they would never do under any other circumstance. It can also occur when they could not save a buddy—even when the expectation is completely unrealistic. It is powerful in a victim of domestic violence who frequently is told she is the cause of the violence with such statements supported by twisting Scripture.

In my experience the deep struggles of the soul cannot truly be considered until the trauma victim has experienced a relationship that bears the fragrance of

Christ in hard places. We need the Word made flesh first. We also need some of the darkness illuminated so we understand the lies that have been wrapped around our souls from the evil done to us. Then the questions about God and who he is come and the ground is plowed for a much deeper understanding of the work of Christ on the cross. He knows the depth of the evil done; he has borne the great sorrows; he has been wounded so that we might be healed.

I send my clients on a search to uncover that the cross of Christ is God with us—in our sin, our suffering, our grief, and our sorrow. When trauma victims are struggling with spiritual questions, I often direct them to a particular passage or raise a specific question. Rather than simply teaching them I send them to study and learn. The work has far more power when they wrestle with it themselves. This is *not* something I do early on in therapy—it falls more toward the end of the second phase and into the third.[5] One of the reasons I wait is that many times people who have experienced child sexual abuse or relentless or overwhelming trauma come into counseling with some very confused spiritual ideas that will govern any work we try to do. Another of the major reasons for this is that I find they will grasp the profound truths of the cross far more readily and deeply if they have seen some representation of those truths in their relationship with me. They have been able to speak the unspeakable. They are known. They are loved. No matter what they tell, they remain safe. I can forgive. I have hope for them. Out of that experience in flesh and blood, they can then turn to the person and work of Christ and his identification with them. I have without exception found it a powerful way of teaching truth and of bringing healing.

Endnotes

[1] N. Postman & C. Weingartner, *Teaching as a Subversive Activity* (New York: Delacorte Press, 1969).

[2] Jeffrey Fleishman, "He Left Bosnia for Mount Airy. But His Heart Stayed Behind. Coming Home to the Ruins of War," *The Philadelphia Inquirer*, October 14, 1997.

[3] Roy Baumeister, *Evil: Inside Human Violence and Cruelty* (New York: Henry Holt, 1999), 141.

[4] Klaas Schilder, *Christ Crucified* (St. Catherines, ON: Paideia Press, 1979).

[5] Diane Langberg, "Chapter 14: Complex Trauma," *Suffering and the Heart of God*, (Greensboro, NC: New Growth Press, 2015). This chapter provides a fuller discussion of treatment phases.